ALL ABOUT YOU

ALL ABOUT YOU

By Gail Mahan

Illustrated by Merrily Mihel

HALLMARK EDITIONS

ALL ABOUT YOU

A little book to open
when you're all alone,
and nobody's looking . . .

Full of praise for all
you are and do,
when nobody's looking . . .

For you, medals!

Medals for the nice
deeds you've done
that no one noticed . . .

Medals for the times you cared
when no one else did...

Medals for the times you helped
and no one knew.

For you, ribbons!

Ribbons for trying to grow
a little bigger every day...

Ribbons for trying new things
and discovering new ways . . .

Ribbons for magnificent dreams
you dare to dream.

Prizes for you!

Prizes for always
hearing with your heart...

Prizes for seeing good things
in the world
that others may miss...

Prizes for warming those
who need you near
when others go their way.

Roses for you!

Roses for making others happy
by doing happy things . . .

Roses for your laughter
that lightens someone s heart...

Roses for always being dearer
than you could ever know!

And especially, love for you!

Love for you,
because somebody knows
how very, very nice you are . . .

Even when nobody's looking.